Preface

Welcome to the world of English Olympiad MCQ With Solutions Class 4. We're thrilled to have you start this journey, which will open doors to new experiences, ideas, and connections. English is more than just a subject in school—it's a valuable skill that can enhance every part of your life, from making friends to exploring cultures, watching movies, and even navigating the internet. With English, you gain a tool to connect with people worldwide, express your thoughts clearly, and explore the richness of global literature, media, and knowledge.

This book is designed to make learning English enjoyable, practical, and comprehensive. Whether you're new to the language or have some experience, each chapter will guide you in mastering vocabulary, grammar, speaking, reading, writing, and listening skills. Through engaging stories, relatable characters, and fun activities, this book helps you see English in action and understand its power as a language of communication, creativity, and expression.

We follow the principles of the **National Education Policy (NEP) 2020**, which emphasises holistic, competency-based, and enjoyable learning. The NEP encourages practical skills, critical thinking, and meaningful engagement, and this book is designed to meet these goals. With every lesson, you'll build valuable competencies in academics and real-world situations. We've included activities and scenarios that bring English to life, from simple conversations to meaningful self-expression.

Additionally, we have integrated lessons that connect with the **Sustainable Development Goals (SDGs)**, such as Quality Education, Gender Equality, Climate Action, and Peace and Justice. These goals encourage students to understand global challenges and work toward a better world. By learning English in this international context, you'll gain language skills and become more aware of how to contribute positively to the world.

As you read the book, remember that language learning is a gradual journey. Practice regularly, celebrate your progress, and enjoy the process. With each chapter, you'll discover the joy of expressing yourself, learning about new topics, and connecting with the world through English. We hope this book becomes a helpful companion in your journey. Happy learning!

Table of Contents

Preface 1

Chapter 1 - Wake Up! 3

Chapter 2 -Neha's Alarm Clock 8

Chapter 3 -Noses 13

Chapter 4 - The Little Fir Tree 18

Chapter 5 - Run! 23

Chapter 6 - Nasruddin's Aim 28

Chapter 7 - Why? 33

Chapter 8 - Alice in Wonderland 38

Chapter 9 - Don't Be Afraid of the Dark 43

Chapter 10 - Helen Keller 48

Chapter 11 – Hiawatha 53

Chapter 12 - The Scholar's Mother Tongue 58

Chapter 13 - Watering Rhyme 63

Chapter 14 - The Giving Tree 68

Chapter 15 – Books 73

Chapter 16 - Going to Buy a Book 78

Chapter 17 - The Naughty Boy 83

Chapter 1 - Wake Up!

Q1 What is the poem “Wake Up!” about?

a) Sleeping late

b) Waking up early

c) Playing at night

d) Dreaming

Answer: b) Waking up early

Q2 Who is the poet encouraging to wake up?

a) Animals

b) The reader

c) Birds

d) Trees

Answer: b) The reader

Q3 What does the poet want us to see in the morning?

a) The rising sun

b) The stars

c) The moon

d) The rain

Answer: a) The rising sun

Q4 Which animals are mentioned as being awake in the morning?

a) The cows and horses

b) The birds and bees

c) The cats and dogs

d) The lions and tigers

Answer: b) The birds and bees

Q5 How does the poet describe the morning?

a) Dark and quiet

b) Bright and cheerful

c) Rainy and stormy

d) Snowy and cold

Answer: b) Bright and cheerful

Q6 What does the poet encourage us to do after waking up?

a) Go for a walk

b) Go back to sleep

c) Stay indoors

d) Dance and sing

Answer: a) Go for a walk

Q7 Why does the poet want us to wake up early?

a) To enjoy the beauty of the morning

b) To complete homework

c) To clean the house

d) To cook food

Answer: a) To enjoy the beauty of the morning

Q8 What does the poet suggest is a benefit of waking up early?

a) Seeing the world come alive

b) Getting more sleep

c) Avoiding work

d) Eating a lot

Answer: a) Seeing the world come alive

Q9 What sound does the poet mention in the poem?

a) Birds singing

b) Dogs barking

c) Cars honking

d) People talking

Answer: a) Birds singing

Q10 What does the poet want us to feel in the morning?

a) Happy and energetic

b) Sad and tired

c) Angry

d) Lazy

Answer: a) Happy and energetic

Q11 Who wakes up along with the poet in the morning?

a) The birds

b) The stars

c) The clouds

d) The moon

Answer: a) The birds

Q12 What colour does the poet associate with the morning?

a) Bright and colourful

b) Dark and gloomy

c) Gray and dull

d) Black and white

Answer: a) Bright and colourful

Q13 How does the morning make the poet feel?

a) Excited and joyful

b) Nervous

c) Scared

d) Angry

Answer: a) Excited and joyful

Q14 According to the poem, what do the bees do in the morning?

a) Fly around and buzz

b) Sleep

c) Hide in flowers

d) Dance in the rain

Answer: a) Fly around and buzz

Q15 What is the poet's attitude toward waking up early?

a) Positive and encouraging

b) Sad and reluctant

c) Confused

d) Angry

Answer: a) Positive and encouraging

Q16 The poet compares the morning to a time that is

a) Full of life and energy

b) Calm and silent

c) Busy and stressful

d) Dark and gloomy

Answer: a) Full of life and energy

Q17 What does the poet encourage readers to do besides waking up?

a) Be active and enjoy nature

b) Stay inside

c) Go back to bed

d) Play video games

Answer: a) Be active and enjoy nature

Q18 What do the birds and bees symbolize in the poem?

a) The beauty of nature and morning life

b) The need for rest

c) The quiet of the night

d) The darkness of winter

Answer: a) The beauty of nature and morning life

Q19 The phrase "Wake Up!" in the poem is meant to inspire

a) Excitement to start the day

b) A sense of boredom

c) A feeling of fear

d) Laziness

Answer: a) Excitement to start the day

Q20 What does the poet want us to appreciate by waking up early?

a) The beauty of the natural world around us

b) The quiet of the night

c) The peace of sleeping in

d) The fun of staying indoors

Answer: a) The beauty of the natural world around us

Chapter 2 -Neha's Alarm Clock

Q1 What usually wakes Neha up in the morning?

a) Her mother

b) Her alarm clock

c) Her father

d) Her pet dog

Answer: b) Her alarm clock

Q2 What sound does Neha's alarm clock make?

a) Tick-tock

b) Buzz-buzz

c) Ring-ring

d) Ding-dong

Answer: c) Ring-ring

Q3 Why does Neha dislike her alarm clock?

a) It wakes her up too early

b) It is broken

c) It doesn't make any noise

d) It is too quiet

Answer: a) It wakes her up too early

Q4 What happens to the alarm clock one day?

a) It stops working

b) It gets louder

c) It falls off the table

d) It rings all day

Answer: a) It stops working

Q5 How does Neha wake up when the alarm clock stops working?

a) The sun's rays wake her up

b) Her mother wakes her up

c) She wakes up late

d) She does not wake up

Answer: a) The sun's rays wake her up

Q6 Who tries to wake Neha up when the alarm clock doesn't work?

a) The birds

b) The dog

c) Her mother

d) Her friend

Answer: a) The birds

Q7 What does Neha wish she could do?

a) Sleep longer

b) Wake up early

c) Go to school on time

d) Play all day

Answer: a) Sleep longer

Q8 How does the sun wake Neha up?

a) By shining in her eyes

b) By making a sound

c) By pulling her blanket

d) By calling her name

Answer: a) By shining in her eyes

Q9 Who else tries to wake Neha up?

a) The school bell

b) The birds

c) Her father

d) Her pet cat

Answer: b) The birds

Q10 How does Neha feel about waking up early?

a) She dislikes it

b) She loves it

c) She feels excited

d) She feels proud

Answer: a) She dislikes it

Q11 When the alarm clock and the sun fail, who finally wakes her up?

a) Her body's natural clock

b) Her teacher

c) Her friends

d) Her pet dog

Answer: a) Her body's natural clock

Q12 What lesson does Neha learn at the end?

a) Her body can wake her up without an alarm

b) She needs a new alarm clock

c) She should stay up late

d) Her parents will always wake her up

Answer: a) Her body can wake her up without an alarm

Q13 What is Neha's favorite thing to do in the morning?

a) Sleep a bit more

b) Go for a walk

c) Have breakfast

d) Do her homework

Answer: a) Sleep a bit more

Q14 What does Neha realize about waking up?

a) She doesn't need an alarm clock

b) She should wake up very early

c) She likes the alarm clock

d) She needs her mom to wake her

Answer: a) She doesn't need an alarm clock

Q15 Neha feels that waking up naturally is

a) Relaxing

b) Annoying

c) Boring

d) Scary

Answer: a) Relaxing

Q16 Who helps Neha understand that she doesn't need an alarm?

a) Her own body

b) Her mother

c) Her friend

d) Her teacher

Answer: a) Her own body

Q17 What is the moral of the story?

a) Our body has its own natural clock

b) Alarm clocks are essential

c) Sleeping late is good

d) Waking up is always difficult

Answer: a) Our body has its own natural clock

Q18 Neha's routine in the morning shows the importance of

a) A natural sleep-wake cycle

b) Staying in bed

c) Being lazy

d) Forgetting responsibilities

Answer: a) A natural sleep-wake cycle

Q19 Neha's alarm clock is symbolic of

a) Dependence on external help

b) Love for mornings

c) School discipline

d) Enjoying the day

Answer: a) Dependence on external help

Q20 At the end of the story, Neha learns to

a) Trust her body’s natural rhythm

b) Buy a new alarm clock

c) Sleep longer every day

d) Rely on others to wake her

Answer: a) Trust her body’s natural rhythm

Chapter 3 -Noses

Q1 What is the poem "Noses" about?

a) Different shapes of noses

b) The beauty of noses

c) People's opinions on noses

d) A girl admiring her nose

Answer: d) A girl admiring her nose

Q2 How does the girl feel about her nose?

a) Amused

b) Angry

c) Disappointed

d) Confused

Answer: a) Amused

Q3 The girl describes her nose as

a) Funny

b) Long

c) Wide

d) Short

Answer: a) Funny

Q4 Where does the girl look at her nose?

a) In the mirror

b) In a book

c) In the window

d) In a picture

Answer: a) In the mirror

Q5 What shape does the girl compare her nose to?

a) A little button

b) A big circle

c) A straight line

d) A triangle

Answer: a) A little button

Q6 How does the girl feel while looking at her nose?

a) Happy and amused

b) Sad and embarrassed

c) Angry and annoyed

d) Proud and confident

Answer: a) Happy and amused

Q7 The poem describes the nose as

a) A little funny feature

b) A big and serious part

c) An invisible part

d) A silent object

Answer: a) A little funny feature

Q8 What does the girl think her nose looks like?

a) A funny shape

b) A long stick

c) A big nose

d) A small line

Answer: a) A funny shape

Q9 Why does the girl enjoy looking at her nose?

a) Because it looks funny

b) Because it's big

c) Because it's very small

d) Because it's invisible

Answer: a) Because it looks funny

Q10 What does the girl feel about having a nose?

a) It's special and unique

b) It’s boring

c) It’s unnecessary

d) It’s a problem

Answer: a) It’s special and unique

Q11 How does the poem make the reader feel about noses?

a) They are funny and special

b) They are embarrassing

c) They are annoying

d) They are scary

Answer: a) They are funny and special

Q12 What is the girl’s attitude towards her nose?

a) Positive and playful

b) Disappointed

c) Nervous

d) Scared

Answer: a) Positive and playful

Q13 How does the poem suggest people feel about their own noses?

a) They find them funny and unique

b) They don’t care about them

c) They are embarrassed

d) They dislike them

Answer: a) They find them funny and unique

Q14 The girl in the poem feels that her nose

a) Makes her look unique

b) Should be hidden

c) Is too big

d) Is too small

Answer: a) Makes her look unique

Q15 How does the girl view her nose in comparison to others?

a) As something to laugh about

b) As something to hide

c) As something very large

d) As something very small

Answer: a) As something to laugh about

Q16 The poem "Noses" encourages us to

a) Embrace our unique features

b) Ignore our appearance

c) Worry about our looks

d) Change our features

Answer: a) Embrace our unique features

Q17 The girl's attitude towards her nose is best described as

a) Proud and cheerful

b) Nervous

c) Scared

d) Annoyed

Answer: a) Proud and cheerful

Q18 The poem uses the girl's nose to show

a) The humor in our appearance

b) Fear of being different

c) Anger at looks

d) Boredom with life

Answer: a) The humor in our appearance

Q19 What does the poem say about everyone's nose?

a) It's special in its own way

b) It's the same

c) It's boring

d) It's annoying

Answer: a) It's special in its own way

Q20 The poem "Noses" teaches us to

a) Appreciate ourselves

b) Feel embarrassed

c) Hide our noses

d) Ignore our appearance

Answer: a) Appreciate ourselves

Chapter 4 - The Little Fir Tree

Q1 Who is the main character in the story?

a) A fir tree

b) A boy

c) A magician

d) A fairy

Answer: a) A fir tree

Q2 What was the fir tree unhappy about in the beginning?

a) Its height

b) Its needles

c) Its color

d) Its shape

Answer: b) Its needles

Q3 Who granted the fir tree's wishes?

a) A fairy

b) A magician

c) A shepherd

d) A woodcutter

Answer: b) A magician

Q4 What did the fir tree wish for first?

a) Green leaves

b) Golden leaves

c) Silver leaves

d) Long branches

Answer: b) Golden leaves

Q5 What happened to the golden leaves?

a) They were stolen

b) They fell off

c) They turned green

d) They were eaten by animals

Answer: a) They were stolen

Q6 After losing the golden leaves, what did the fir tree wish for?

a) Silver leaves

b) New branches

c) Green leaves

d) Long roots

Answer: a) Silver leaves

Q7 What happened to the silver leaves?

a) They were taken by the wind

b) They were eaten by goats

c) They turned gold

d) They grew bigger

Answer: b) They were eaten by goats

Q8 What was the fir tree's next wish?

a) Glass leaves

b) Green leaves

c) Blue flowers

d) Fruits

Answer: a) Glass leaves

Q9 What happened to the glass leaves?

a) They broke in the wind

b) They turned to gold

c) They grew back

d) They turned green

Answer: a) They broke in the wind

Q10 What was the fir tree's final wish?

a) To have its original leaves back

b) To have green, shiny leaves

c) To grow flowers

d) To stay small

Answer: a) To have its original leaves back

Q11 How did the fir tree feel after getting its original leaves back?

a) Happy and content

b) Sad and disappointed

c) Angry and annoyed

d) Scared and worried

Answer: a) Happy and content

Q12 What lesson does the story teach?

a) Be happy with who you are

b) Change is always good

c) Being rich is important

d) Wishes are always granted

Answer: a) Be happy with who you are

Q13 Who helped the fir tree learn a valuable lesson?

a) The magician

b) A bird

c) The animals

d) The wind

Answer: a) The magician

Q14 The fir tree's wishes were driven by

a) Discontent with itself

b) Pride

c) Anger

d) Happiness

Answer: a) Discontent with itself

Q15 The story teaches us the value of

a) Self-acceptance

b) Wealth

c) Popularity

d) Strength

Answer: a) Self-acceptance

Q16 What did the fir tree learn from its experience?

a) To be happy as it is

b) To wish for gold

c) To have silver leaves

d) To keep wishing

Answer: a) To be happy as it is

Q17 How did the fir tree feel after its first wish was granted?

a) Proud

b) Scared

c) Sad

d) Excited

Answer: d) Excited

Q18 Each wish of the fir tree led to

a) A new problem

b) Lasting happiness

c) More wishes

d) Sadness

Answer: a) A new problem

Q19 The story emphasizes the importance of

a) Accepting oneself

b) Changing constantly

c) Becoming rich

d) Seeking fame

Answer: a) Accepting oneself

Q20 What did the fir tree ultimately decide about its needles?

a) It was happy with them

b) It wanted more wishes

c) It needed golden leaves

d) It disliked them

Answer: a) It was happy with them

Chapter 5 - Run!

Q1 What is the main theme of the poem "Run!"?

a) Enjoying nature and freedom

b) Studying hard

c) Running away from home

d) Sleeping all day

Answer: a) Enjoying nature and freedom

Q2 Where does the poet suggest we should run?

a) In the sun

b) To the hills

c) To the rivers

d) All of the above

Answer: d) All of the above

Q3 What does the poet say to run away from?

a) The city noise

b) The busy streets

c) The sad, gloomy days

d) The house

Answer: c) The sad, gloomy days

Q4 Running brings a feeling of

a) Freedom and joy

b) Sadness

c) Anger

d) Boredom

Answer: a) Freedom and joy

Q5 What does the poet suggest happens when we run around?

a) We feel happier

b) We get bored

c) We feel tired

d) We feel scared

Answer: a) We feel happier

Q6 The poet encourages us to run in

a) The countryside

b) The playground

c) The fields and hills

d) The city

Answer: c) The fields and hills

Q7 What emotion does the poem "Run!" evoke?

a) Happiness

b) Fear

c) Anger

d) Boredom

Answer: a) Happiness

Q8 The poet wants us to enjoy

a) The fresh air

b) The night

c) The rainy day

d) The quiet indoors

Answer: a) The fresh air

Q9 How does running make us feel according to the poem?

a) Light and free

b) Tired and sleepy

c) Sad

d) Angry

Answer: a) Light and free

Q10 The poem "Run!" suggests running as a way to

a) Feel joyful and alive

b) Avoid work

c) Get tired

d) Ignore everything

Answer: a) Feel joyful and alive

Q11 The poet describes running as an activity that brings

a) Joy and freedom

b) Wealth

c) Sadness

d) Frustration

Answer: a) Joy and freedom

Q12 Why does the poet suggest we run through the meadows?

a) To feel close to nature

b) To avoid others

c) To get to school

d) To exercise

Answer: a) To feel close to nature

Q13 The poet encourages running in

a) Fields, hills, and meadows

b) Crowded places

c) Quiet indoors

d) The city

Answer: a) Fields, hills, and meadows

Q14 The poet views running as a way to

a) Release energy and experience happiness

b) Stay tired

c) Feel scared

d) Get sad

Answer: a) Release energy and experience happiness

Q15 Running allows us to experience

a) Freedom and joy

b) Quietness and calm

c) Anger

d) Boredom

Answer: a) Freedom and joy

Q16 Where does the poet suggest to run in the poem?

a) In the fields and hills

b) In the crowded streets

c) Inside the house

d) In the rain

Answer: a) In the fields and hills

Q17 The poem "Run!" inspires readers to

a) Embrace outdoor freedom

b) Stay indoors

c) Get tired

d) Avoid nature

Answer: a) Embrace outdoor freedom

Q18 The tone of the poem "Run!" is

a) Exciting and playful

b) Boring

c) Sad

d) Angry

Answer: a) Exciting and playful

Q19 What does the poet say we can hear while running?

a) Sounds of nature

b) People talking

c) Cars honking

d) Music playing

Answer: a) Sounds of nature

Q20 The poem "Run!" inspires us to connect with

a) Nature and joy

b) Busy city life

c) Staying indoors

d) Sleeping more

Answer: a) Nature and joy

Chapter 6 - Nasruddin's Aim

Q1 What skill is Nasruddin showing off in the story?

a) Archery

b) Sword fighting

c) Swimming

d) Running

Answer: a) Archery

Q2 Who is the main character in the story?

a) Nasruddin

b) The king

c) A young boy

d) Nasruddin's friend

Answer: a) Nasruddin

Q3 What does Nasruddin claim to be the best at?

a) Archery

b) Cooking

c) Dancing

d) Singing

Answer: a) Archery

Q4 What does Nasruddin's friend ask him to prove?

a) That he can hit the target

b) That he can sing well

c) That he can cook

d) That he can fly

Answer: a) That he can hit the target

Q5 How does Nasruddin respond when he misses his first shot?

a) He blames the wind

b) He says it was not his shot

c) He apologizes

d) He tries again immediately

Answer: b) He says it was not his shot

Q6 What excuse does Nasruddin make for his first missed shot?

a) It was someone else's shot

b) The bow was too tight

c) The target was moving

d) It was too windy

Answer: a) It was someone else's shot

Q7 How many times does Nasruddin miss the target?

a) Twice

b) Once

c) Three times

d) Four times

Answer: a) Twice

Q8 What excuse does Nasruddin give for his second miss?

a) He says it was his friend Azad's shot

b) He blames the bow

c) He blames the target

d) He says he was distracted

Answer: a) He says it was his friend Azad's shot

Q9 What finally happens when Nasruddin takes his third shot?

a) He hits the target

b) He misses again

c) He breaks the bow

d) He gives up

Answer: a) He hits the target

Q10 What is Nasruddin's reaction after hitting the target?

a) He is proud and boasts about his skills

b) He laughs

c) He apologizes

d) He gives his bow to someone else

Answer: a) He is proud and boasts about his skills

Q11 How do Nasruddin's friends react when he hits the target?

a) They cheer and clap

b) They leave the place

c) They criticize him

d) They ask him to shoot again

Answer: a) They cheer and clap

Q12 What does the story of Nasruddin's Aim teach us?

a) To laugh at ourselves and not take everything seriously

b) To show off our skills

c) To criticize others

d) To never miss a target

Answer: a) To laugh at ourselves and not take everything seriously

Q13 Nasruddin's attitude when he misses the target is

a) Calm and humorous

b) Angry

c) Sad

d) Scared

Answer: a) Calm and humorous

Q14 The story of Nasruddin's Aim is mostly about

a) Humour and self-confidence

b) Anger and frustration

c) Competition and winning

d) Sadness and loss

Answer: a) Humour and self-confidence

Q15 How does Nasruddin justify his actions?

a) By giving funny excuses

b) By apologizing sincerely

c) By blaming others

d) By arguing with his friends

Answer: a) By giving funny excuses

Q16 How does the story make readers feel about Nasruddin?

a) He is funny and clever

b) He is boring

c) He is angry

d) He is mean

Answer: a) He is funny and clever

Q17 Nasruddin's friends in the story are

a) Amused by his excuses

b) Angry with him

c) Bored

d) Ignoring him

Answer: a) Amused by his excuses

Q18 The story of Nasruddin's Aim encourages us to

a) Take life lightly and have a sense of humour

b) Be serious all the time

c) Not make any mistakes

d) Show off our skills always

Answer: a) Take life lightly and have a sense of humour

Q19 What does Nasruddin claim when he finally hits the target?

a) That it was his own shot

b) That it was Azad's shot

c) That it was a lucky shot

d) That he missed it

Answer: a) That it was his own shot

Q20 The lesson in the story is that we should

a) Have confidence but also laugh at ourselves

b) Always hit the target

c) Never laugh at others

d) Be angry at our mistakes

Answer: a) Have confidence but also laugh at ourselves

Chapter 7 - **Why?**

Q1 What is the poem "Why?" about?

a) A child's endless questions

b) A child's dream

c) A child's bedtime

d) A child's morning routine

Answer: a) A child's endless questions

Q2 What kind of questions does the child ask in the poem?

a) Questions about nature and the world

b) Questions about school

c) Questions about toys

d) Questions about homework

Answer: a) Questions about nature and the world

Q3 What does the child want to know about the moon?

a) Why it shines

b) Why it hides

c) Why it moves

d) Why it is round

Answer: a) Why it shines

Q4 The child's questions in the poem show

a) Curiosity about the world

b) Fear of the dark

c) Happiness

d) Laziness

Answer: a) Curiosity about the world

Q5 What does the child wonder about flowers?

a) Why they have color

b) Why they grow

c) Why they smell

d) Why they are big

Answer: a) Why they have color

Q6 What question does the child ask about birds?

a) Why they sing

b) Why they fly

c) Why they sleep

d) Why they eat

Answer: b) Why they fly

Q7 The poem reflects the child's natural

a) Wonder and curiosity

b) Anger and frustration

c) Sadness and worry

d) Fear and doubt

Answer: a) Wonder and curiosity

Q8 Why does the child ask questions in the poem?

a) To understand the world better

b) To make friends

c) To complete homework

d) To avoid studying

Answer: a) To understand the world better

Q9 The child's questions are

a) Endless and imaginative

b) Boring

c) Scary

d) Unimportant

Answer: a) Endless and imaginative

Q10 What does the child wonder about rain?

a) Why it falls

b) Why it is cold

c) Why it comes at night

d) Why it is loud

Answer: a) Why it falls

Q11 What does the child ask about fish?

a) Why they swim

b) Why they fly

c) Why they sing

d) Why they crawl

Answer: a) Why they swim

Q12 What does the child wonder about stars?

a) Why they shine at night

b) Why they are big

c) Why they are loud

d) Why they are colorful

Answer: a) Why they shine at night

Q13 What kind of tone does the poem "Why?" have?

a) Playful and curious

b) Angry and sad

c) Serious and quiet

d) Nervous and scared

Answer: a) Playful and curious

Q14 What does the poem "Why?" encourage in children?

a) To ask questions and be curious

b) To avoid asking questions

c) To ignore nature

d) To be silent

Answer: a) To ask questions and be curious

Q15 The child's questions show a love for

a) Exploring and learning

b) Staying indoors

c) Sleeping

d) Avoiding people

Answer: a) Exploring and learning

Q16 What does the child ask about lightning?

a) Why it flashes

b) Why it is silent

c) Why it is slow

d) Why it is colorful

Answer: a) Why it flashes

Q17 The poem "Why?" suggests that questions help us

a) Learn and grow

b) Stay confused

c) Feel scared

d) Be angry

Answer: a) Learn and grow

Q18 What does the child want to know about leaves?

a) Why they change color

b) Why they fall

c) Why they are big

d) Why they are strong

Answer: a) Why they change color

Q19 What lesson can we learn from the poem?

a) It's okay to be curious and ask questions

b) Questions are annoying

c) We should not be curious

d) The world is too complex to understand

Answer: a) It's okay to be curious and ask questions

Q20 The poem "Why?" encourages readers to

a) Appreciate and explore the wonders of the world

b) Ignore questions

c) Worry about answers

d) Fear new things

Answer: a) Appreciate and explore the wonders of the world

Chapter 8 - Alice in Wonderland

Q1 Who is the main character in the story?

a) Alice

b) The White Rabbit

c) The Queen

d) The Caterpillar

Answer: a) Alice

Q2 What catches Alice's attention at the beginning of the story?

a) A White Rabbit with a pocket watch

b) A flower talking

c) A giant mushroom

d) A treasure chest

Answer: a) A White Rabbit with a pocket watch

Q3 What is unusual about the White Rabbit?

a) It talks and wears clothes

b) It has blue fur

c) It flies

d) It can sing

Answer: a) It talks and wears clothes

Q4 What does Alice do when she sees the White Rabbit?

a) She follows it down a rabbit hole

b) She calls for help

c) She catches it

d) She ignores it

Answer: a) She follows it down a rabbit hole

Q5 Where does Alice find herself after following the rabbit?

a) In Wonderland

b) In her garden

c) In a city

d) In a school

Answer: a) In Wonderland

Q6 How does Alice feel when she first enters Wonderland?

a) Curious and excited

b) Angry

c) Tired

d) Scared

Answer: a) Curious and excited

Q7 Who does Alice meet in Wonderland?

a) Strange creatures and characters

b) Only her friends

c) Only animals

d) Only people

Answer: a) Strange creatures and characters

Q8 What does Alice drink that changes her size?

a) A magical potion

b) Water

c) Milk

d) Juice

Answer: a) A magical potion

Q9 How does the magical potion affect Alice?

a) She grows bigger or smaller

b) She becomes invisible

c) She becomes very fast

d) She can fly

Answer: a) She grows bigger or smaller

Q10 What is the name of the land Alice enters?

a) Wonderland

b) Fairyland

c) Dreamland

d) Magicland

Answer: a) Wonderland

Q11 Alice's adventures in Wonderland represent

a) Her imagination and curiosity

b) Her fears

c) Her anger

d) Her sadness

Answer: a) Her imagination and curiosity

Q12 Who tells Alice to hurry in Wonderland?

a) The White Rabbit

b) The Queen

c) The Caterpillar

d) The Mouse

Answer: a) The White Rabbit

Q13 Why is Wonderland different from Alice's real world?

a) It is magical and filled with talking animals

b) It is very quiet

c) It has no people

d) It is very dark

Answer: a) It is magical and filled with talking animals

Q14 What does Alice's journey in Wonderland teach her?

a) To embrace curiosity and adventure

b) To avoid animals

c) To never follow strangers

d) To always stay home

Answer: a) To embrace curiosity and adventure

Q15 Who is one of the strange characters Alice meets in Wonderland?

a) The Cheshire Cat

b) A giant spider

c) A flying lion

d) A magical tree

Answer: a) The Cheshire Cat

Q16 What does Alice find challenging in Wonderland?

a) The constantly changing surroundings

b) The quietness

c) The darkness

d) The lack of food

Answer: a) The constantly changing surroundings

Q17 What kind of story is "Alice in Wonderland"?

a) A fantasy adventure

b) A mystery

c) A fairy tale

d) A horror story

Answer: a) A fantasy adventure

Q18 Alice's adventures in Wonderland help her explore

a) Her imagination and creativity

b) Her fears and anger

c) Her laziness

d) Her sadness

Answer: a) Her imagination and creativity

Q19 Why is Alice curious about the rabbit?

a) Because it talks and wears clothes

b) Because it is very large

c) Because it is glowing

d) Because it is silent

Answer: a) Because it talks and wears clothes

Q20 The story of "Alice in Wonderland" encourages readers to

a) Follow their curiosity and be open to new adventures

b) Avoid new things

c) Be afraid of strangers

d) Ignore strange events

Answer: a) Follow their curiosity and be open to new adventures

Chapter 9 - Don’t Be Afraid of the Dark

Q1 What is the main theme of the poem "Don’t Be Afraid of the Dark"?

a) Overcoming fear of darkness

b) Being angry at night

c) Studying hard

d) Ignoring the dark

Answer: a) Overcoming fear of darkness

Q2 What does the poet encourage children to do?

a) Embrace and not fear the dark

b) Ignore the dark

c) Always stay indoors

d) Sleep all day

Answer: a) Embrace and not fear the dark

Q3 According to the poem, what is the dark like?

a) A friend

b) A scary monster

c) A stranger

d) An enemy

Answer: a) A friend

Q4 What time of day does the poem focus on?

a) Night

b) Morning

c) Afternoon

d) Evening

Answer: a) Night

Q5 What does the poet say hides in the dark?

a) Stars and the moon

b) Scary monsters

c) Ghosts

d) Loud noises

Answer: a) Stars and the moon

Q6 What does the poet want children to understand about the dark?

a) It is peaceful and calming

b) It is dangerous

c) It is loud and noisy

d) It is confusing

Answer: a) It is peaceful and calming

Q7 What shines in the dark according to the poem?

a) Stars and the moon

b) Flowers

c) Birds

d) Clouds

Answer: a) Stars and the moon

Q8 How does the poet describe the night?

a) Gentle and calm

b) Rough and scary

c) Loud and noisy

d) Sad and dull

Answer: a) Gentle and calm

Q9 What does the poet suggest we do at night?

a) Sleep peacefully

b) Stay awake

c) Be afraid

d) Hide

Answer: a) Sleep peacefully

Q10 What do children often feel about the dark according to the poem?

a) Scared and nervous

b) Excited

c) Happy

d) Calm

Answer: a) Scared and nervous

Q11 The poem helps children understand that darkness is

a) Safe and friendly

b) Dangerous

c) Unwanted

d) Annoying

Answer: a) Safe and friendly

Q12 What does the poet say the dark is full of?

a) Stars and beauty

b) Sadness

c) Anger

d) Noise

Answer: a) Stars and beauty

Q13 The poem encourages children to feel

a) Calm and peaceful at night

b) Worried

c) Angry

d) Nervous

Answer: a) Calm and peaceful at night

Q14 What shines brightly in the night sky?

a) The moon and stars

b) Birds

c) The sun

d) Flowers

Answer: a) The moon and stars

Q15 What does the poet compare the dark to?

a) A friend who is gentle

b) A stranger

c) A problem

d) A scary animal

Answer: a) A friend who is gentle

Q16 The poem "Don’t Be Afraid of the Dark" tells children that the dark is

a) Gentle and safe

b) Dangerous

c) Scary

d) Loud

Answer: a) Gentle and safe

Q17 According to the poet, how should children feel at bedtime?

a) Calm and secure

b) Scared

c) Sad

d) Angry

Answer: a) Calm and secure

Q18 What is the poem’s main message?

a) Not to fear the dark

b) To always stay indoors

c) To sleep in the day

d) To avoid stars

Answer: a) Not to fear the dark

Q19 The poem suggests that darkness is

a) Beautiful and full of wonders

b) Boring

c) Dangerous

d) Scary

Answer: a) Beautiful and full of wonders

Q20 The poet wants children to view the dark as

a) A friend, not an enemy

b) A stranger

c) A problem

d) A danger

Answer: a) A friend, not an enemy

Chapter 10 - Helen Keller

Q1 Who is the main character in the story?

a) Helen Keller

b) Anne Sullivan

c) Helen's mother

d) Helen's friend

Answer: a) Helen Keller

Q2 What was Helen Keller unable to do?

a) See and hear

b) Walk

c) Speak clearly

d) Run fast

Answer: a) See and hear

Q3 At what age did Helen lose her ability to see and hear?

a) When she was a baby

b) At the age of two

c) When she was a teenager

d) In her twenties

Answer: b) At the age of two

Q4 Who helped Helen learn to communicate?

a) Anne Sullivan

b) Her father

c) A doctor

d) Her sister

Answer: a) Anne Sullivan

Q5 What was the first word Helen learned?

a) Water

b) Food

c) Love

d) Tree

Answer: a) Water

Q6 How did Anne Sullivan teach Helen to understand words?

a) By spelling words in her hand

b) By showing her pictures

c) By reading books to her

d) By using loud sounds

Answer: a) By spelling words in her hand

Q7 What challenge did Helen face while learning?

a) She couldn't see or hear

b) She was shy

c) She was afraid of water

d) She didn't like studying

Answer: a) She couldn't see or hear

Q8 What did Helen Keller achieve despite her disabilities?

a) She graduated from college

b) She became an artist

c) She traveled the world

d) She became a teacher

Answer: a) She graduated from college

Q9 Helen Keller is an inspiration because she

a) Overcame her disabilities and achieved success

b) Was very wealthy

c) Was the youngest person to graduate

d) Lived in a big house

Answer: a) Overcame her disabilities and achieved success

Q10 Who is known as Helen's "miracle worker"?

a) Anne Sullivan

b) Her father

c) Her sister

d) Her teacher

Answer: a) Anne Sullivan

Q11 Helen's story teaches us about

a) Perseverance and determination

b) Fame and wealth

c) Power and control

d) Luck and chance

Answer: a) Perseverance and determination

Q12 How did Helen feel when she first understood the word "water"?

a) Happy and excited

b) Scared

c) Confused

d) Sad

Answer: a) Happy and excited

Q13 Helen Keller learned to read by

a) Using Braille

b) Listening to tapes

c) Watching TV

d) Writing on paper

Answer: a) Using Braille

Q14 What made Helen's life different from others?

a) She couldn't see or hear

b) She could run very fast

c) She had many siblings

d) She loved to sing

Answer: a) She couldn't see or hear

Q15 What was the most important lesson Helen's life teaches us?

a) We can overcome any obstacle with determination

b) We should only rely on others

c) We should avoid learning

d) We should follow others

Answer: a) We can overcome any obstacle with determination

Q16 Anne Sullivan was not only a teacher but also a

a) Friend and guide to Helen

b) Neighbor

c) Doctor

d) Relative

Answer: a) Friend and guide to Helen

Q17 What skill did Helen master with Anne's help?

a) Communicating and understanding words

b) Singing

c) Dancing

d) Painting

Answer: a) Communicating and understanding words

Q18 Helen Keller's story is an example of

a) Courage and resilience

b) Laziness

c) Fear

d) Anger

Answer: a) Courage and resilience

Q19 Helen Keller's journey teaches us the value of

a) Persistence and hard work

b) Taking shortcuts

c) Having many friends

d) Avoiding challenges

Answer: a) Persistence and hard work

Q20 Helen Keller's life story inspires people to

a) Believe in themselves and never give up

b) Fear challenges

c) Stay away from hard work

d) Take the easy way out

Answer: a) Believe in themselves and never give up

Chapter 11 – **Hiawatha**

Q1 Who is Hiawatha in the poem?

a) A young Native American boy

b) A brave warrior

c) A hunter

d) A fisherman

Answer: a) A young Native American boy

Q2 What is Hiawatha's favorite activity?

a) Observing nature and animals

b) Dancing

c) Singing

d) Building huts

Answer: a) Observing nature and animals

Q3 Who taught Hiawatha about nature?

a) His grandmother Nokomis

b) His mother

c) His father

d) His sister

Answer: a) His grandmother Nokomis

Q4 How does Hiawatha feel about animals?

a) He loves and respects them

b) He fears them

c) He avoids them

d) He hunts them

Answer: a) He loves and respects them

Q5 What does Hiawatha learn from Nokomis?

a) The language of birds and animals

b) How to build fires

c) How to climb trees

d) How to travel

Answer: a) The language of birds and animals

Q6 How does Hiawatha communicate with animals?

a) By understanding their language

b) By giving them food

c) By singing to them

d) By making loud noises

Answer: a) By understanding their language

Q7 What does Hiawatha call the animals?

a) His friends and companions

b) His rivals

c) His enemies

d) Strangers

Answer: a) His friends and companions

Q8 How does Hiawatha feel about birds?

a) He admires them

b) He is afraid of them

c) He ignores them

d) He hunts them

Answer: a) He admires them

Q9 What is Nokomis's relationship with Hiawatha?

a) She is his grandmother

b) She is his mother

c) She is his sister

d) She is his friend

Answer: a) She is his grandmother

Q10 What does the poem reveal about Hiawatha's character?

a) He is kind and close to nature

b) He is angry

c) He is lazy

d) He is lonely

Answer: a) He is kind and close to nature

Q11 Hiawatha's ability to understand animals shows his

a) Deep connection with nature

b) Anger

c) Laziness

d) Fear

Answer: a) Deep connection with nature

Q12 How does Hiawatha feel when he hears the birds sing?

a) Happy and peaceful

b) Sad

c) Bored

d) Scared

Answer: a) Happy and peaceful

Q13 The poem "Hiawatha" is mainly about

a) A boy's relationship with nature

b) A hunting adventure

c) Building a house

d) A fishing trip

Answer: a) A boy's relationship with nature

Q14 Who teaches Hiawatha important lessons about life?

a) His grandmother Nokomis

b) His teacher

c) His father

d) His friend

Answer: a) His grandmother Nokomis

Q15 What is one of the key themes of the poem?

a) Harmony with nature

b) Fighting with animals

c) Avoiding nature

d) Sleeping all day

Answer: a) Harmony with nature

Q16 What does Hiawatha's connection to animals teach us?

a) The importance of respecting all living things

b) The importance of hunting animals

c) To fear animals

d) To ignore animals

Answer: a) The importance of respecting all living things

Q17 Hiawatha learns about the language of

a) Birds and animals

b) People from other villages

c) Stars and moon

d) Trees and rivers

Answer: a) Birds and animals

Q18 Hiawatha's story encourages readers to

a) Appreciate and connect with nature

b) Be fearful of animals

c) Stay away from forests

d) Ignore birds

Answer: a) Appreciate and connect with nature

Q19 What does Hiawatha call the trees?

a) His friends

b) His rivals

c) His enemies

d) His family

Answer: a) His friends

Q20 The poem "Hiawatha" highlights the importance of

a) Living in harmony with nature

b) Building big homes

c) Becoming a hunter

d) Avoiding the forest

Answer: a) Living in harmony with nature

Chapter 12 - The Scholar's Mother Tongue

Q1 Who is the main character in the story?

a) A young scholar

b) A king

c) A farmer

d) A merchant

Answer: a) A young scholar

Q2 What is the young scholar proud of?

a) His knowledge of many languages

b) His singing skills

c) His strength

d) His family wealth

Answer: a) His knowledge of many languages

Q3 What does the king decide to test?

a) The scholar's true mother tongue

b) The scholar's intelligence

c) The scholar's courage

d) The scholar's kindness

Answer: a) The scholar's true mother tongue

Q4 Why does the king want to find out the scholar's mother tongue?

a) He is curious to know if the scholar is truthful

b) He wants to test his own knowledge

c) He dislikes the scholar

d) He wants to make the scholar his minister

Answer: a) He is curious to know if the scholar is truthful

Q5 How does the king plan to find out the scholar's mother tongue?

a) By scaring him at night

b) By giving him a hard test

c) By making him eat spicy food

d) By giving him a puzzle

Answer: a) By scaring him at night

Q6 What does the scholar claim he can speak fluently?

a) Many different languages

b) Only one language

c) Sign language

d) None of the languages

Answer: a) Many different languages

Q7 When the scholar is frightened, he speaks in

a) His mother tongue

b) The king's language

c) A foreign language

d) Sign language

Answer: a) His mother tongue

Q8 What does the king discover about the scholar?

a) His true mother tongue

b) His favorite language

c) His weakness

d) His lack of knowledge

Answer: a) His true mother tongue

Q9 How does the king make the scholar reveal his mother tongue?

a) By suddenly scaring him

b) By asking him politely

c) By bribing him

d) By punishing him

Answer: a) By suddenly scaring him

Q10 Why does the scholar speak in his mother tongue when frightened?

a) It's the language he learned first

b) It's the only language he knows

c) It's the king's favorite language

d) He forgot all other languages

Answer: a) It's the language he learned first

Q11 What is the lesson in "The Scholar's Mother Tongue"?

a) Our true nature often reveals itself under stress

b) Knowledge of many languages is not important

c) It's best to stay quiet

d) Speaking one language is best

Answer: a) Our true nature often reveals itself under stress

Q12 How does the king feel after discovering the scholar's mother tongue?

a) Satisfied and happy

b) Angry

c) Disappointed

d) Surprised

Answer: a) Satisfied and happy

Q13 The story teaches that our mother tongue

a) Is deeply connected to our identity

b) Is not important

c) Can be easily changed

d) Should be hidden

Answer: a) Is deeply connected to our identity

Q14 What was the scholar's reaction when he was scared?

a) He instinctively spoke in his mother tongue

b) He ran away

c) He fought back

d) He started crying

Answer: a) He instinctively spoke in his mother tongue

Q15 Who helped the king to scare the scholar?

a) His minister

b) The queen

c) His guards

d) The scholar's family

Answer: c) His guards

Q16 The king wanted to know the scholar's mother tongue because

a) He wanted to test the scholar's honesty

b) He wanted to know how many languages he could speak

c) He didn't trust the scholar

d) He was angry at the scholar

Answer: a) He wanted to test the scholar's honesty

Q17 What does the story suggest about our first language?

a) It is deeply ingrained in us

b) It can be easily forgotten

c) It is not important

d) It is a sign of intelligence

Answer: a) It is deeply ingrained in us

Q18 The scholar's mother tongue was revealed when he was

a) In a state of fear

b) Writing

c) Eating

d) Speaking to the king

Answer: a) In a state of fear

Q19 The king learned that our mother tongue is

a) Instinctive and comes out naturally

b) Difficult to remember

c) Easily forgotten

d) Not special

Answer: a) Instinctive and comes out naturally

Q20 The story "The Scholar's Mother Tongue" highlights the importance of

a) Embracing our identity

b) Learning many languages

c) Hiding our emotions

d) Avoiding new experiences

Answer: a) Embracing our identity

Chapter 13 - Watering Rhyme

Q1 What is the poem "A Watering Rhyme" about?

a) How to water plants

b) How to play with water

c) How to save water

d) How to grow flowers

Answer: a) How to water plants

Q2 When should we water the plants, according to the poem?

a) Early in the morning or late in the evening

b) In the middle of the day

c) At night only

d) Every hour

Answer: a) Early in the morning or late in the evening

Q3 Why should plants not be watered in the middle of the day?

a) Because it is too hot

b) Because it is too cold

c) Because it is rainy

d) Because it is dark

Answer: a) Because it is too hot

Q4 Watering plants in the heat of the day can

a) Harm the plants

b) Help them grow faster

c) Make them flower immediately

d) Make them produce fruit

Answer: a) Harm the plants

Q5 What does the poet suggest about watering plants?

a) Do it gently and at the right time

b) Do it quickly

c) Do it harshly

d) Avoid it altogether

Answer: a) Do it gently and at the right time

Q6 The best time to water plants is when

a) The sun is not too strong

b) It is raining

c) It is very hot

d) It is very dark

Answer: a) The sun is not too strong

Q7 What can happen if you water plants when the sun is high?

a) It can harm the leaves

b) It can help them bloom

c) It can make them grow faster

d) It can keep them fresh

Answer: a) It can harm the leaves

Q8 The poem gives advice on

a) Caring for plants properly

b) Using a lot of water

c) Ignoring plants

d) Planting new trees

Answer: a) Caring for plants properly

Q9 Watering plants is best done

a) Slowly and gently

b) Very quickly

c) Only once a month

d) With a lot of force

Answer: a) Slowly and gently

Q10 What should you avoid doing while watering plants?

a) Pouring water in the hot sun

b) Pouring water in the morning

c) Using fresh water

d) Watering at sunset

Answer: a) Pouring water in the hot sun

Q11 The poem "A Watering Rhyme" encourages readers to

a) Care for plants responsibly

b) Water plants all the time

c) Ignore plant care

d) Water at random times

Answer: a) Care for plants responsibly

Q12 Why is early morning a good time to water plants?

a) It's cool and refreshing

b) It's very hot

c) There's no sunlight

d) Plants don't need water then

Answer: a) It's cool and refreshing

Q13 The poem teaches us that caring for plants requires

a) The right timing and gentle watering

b) Harsh treatment

c) Ignoring them

d) Cutting their leaves

Answer: a) The right timing and gentle watering

Q14 What should you do if you want plants to grow well?

a) Water them at the right time

b) Avoid watering them

c) Water them all day

d) Water them only in the evening

Answer: a) Water them at the right time

Q15 When watering plants, you should

a) Pour water gently

b) Pour very quickly

c) Use boiling water

d) Pour only a few drops

Answer: a) Pour water gently

Q16 Watering plants at the wrong time can

a) Cause them to wilt

b) Make them flower more

c) Make them grow immediately

d) Keep them fresh

Answer: a) Cause them to wilt

Q17 The poem suggests that plants need water

a) In the morning and evening for best results

b) Only once a week

c) Only at night

d) Anytime during the day

Answer: a) In the morning and evening for best results

Q18 The poem gives advice for taking care of

a) Gardens and plants

b) Cars and bikes

c) Birds and animals

d) Houses and rooms

Answer: a) Gardens and plants

Q19 What should you avoid doing according to the poem?

a) Watering in the hot sun

b) Watering in the morning

c) Giving too little water

d) Watering in the shade

Answer: a) Watering in the hot sun

Q20 The poem "A Watering Rhyme" highlights the importance of

a) Timely and gentle care for plants

b) Watering whenever we want

c) Using a lot of water

d) Ignoring plants

Answer: a) Timely and gentle care for plants

Chapter 14 - The Giving Tree

Q1 Who is the main character in the story "The Giving Tree"?

a) A boy and a tree

b) A girl and a tree

c) A bird and a tree

d) A tree and a river

Answer: a) A boy and a tree

Q2 What does the tree provide for the boy when he is young?

a) Shade and playtime

b) Food and clothes

c) Books and toys

d) Money and a car

Answer: a) Shade and playtime

Q3 What does the boy ask for when he grows up a little?

a) Money

b) A house

c) Fruit from the tree

d) Shade only

Answer: c) Fruit from the tree

Q4 How does the tree feel when the boy takes things from it?

a) Happy to give

b) Sad and hurt

c) Angry

d) Surprised

Answer: a) Happy to give

Q5 What does the boy do with the branches of the tree?

a) Builds a house

b) Sells them

c) Burns them

d) Leaves them on the ground

Answer: a) Builds a house

Q6 How does the tree help the boy when he needs a boat?

a) It gives him its trunk

b) It gives him its roots

c) It tells him to buy one

d) It cannot help him

Answer: a) It gives him its trunk

Q7 What does the tree have left at the end of the story?

a) Only its stump

b) Lots of leaves

c) Fruit

d) Branches and leaves

Answer: a) Only its stump

Q8 How does the boy feel about the tree when he grows old?

a) He appreciates it

b) He forgets about it

c) He feels angry

d) He avoids it

Answer: a) He appreciates it

Q9 What does the boy do with the stump of the tree?

a) Sits and rests on it

b) Climbs it

c) Waters it

d) Cuts it again

Answer: a) Sits and rests on it

Q10 The tree in the story represents

a) Unconditional love and giving

b) Anger and revenge

c) Power and strength

d) Mystery

Answer: a) Unconditional love and giving

Q11 Why does the tree give everything it has to the boy?

a) Because it loves him

b) Because it wants to get rid of him

c) Because it has no other option

d) Because it doesn't like its branches

Answer: a) Because it loves him

Q12 The boy's relationship with the tree teaches us about

a) Selflessness and gratitude

b) Anger and revenge

c) Boredom and laziness

d) Fear and confusion

Answer: a) Selflessness and gratitude

Q13 What is the boy's attitude toward the tree when he is young?

a) He loves and enjoys playing around it

b) He avoids the tree

c) He fears the tree

d) He dislikes the tree

Answer: a) He loves and enjoys playing around it

Q14 What does the boy represent in the story?

a) Human desires and needs

b) Strength

c) Calmness

d) Magic

Answer: a) Human desires and needs

Q15 The tree keeps giving because it wants the boy to

a) Be happy

b) Be angry

c) Stay away

d) Move to a new place

Answer: a) Be happy

Q16 What lesson does the story of "The Giving Tree" teach?

a) The importance of giving without expecting anything in return

b) The importance of keeping things to oneself

c) The joy of fighting

d) The value of taking as much as possible

Answer: a) The importance of giving without expecting anything in return

Q17 How does the story end?

a) The boy sits on the tree stump, finding peace

b) The boy leaves the tree forever

c) The tree grows back

d) The tree falls down

Answer: a) The boy sits on the tree stump, finding peace

Q18 What does the tree give to the boy when he needs shelter?

a) Its branches to build a house

b) Its leaves for food

c) Its fruit for money

d) Its roots

Answer: a) Its branches to build a house

Q19 Why is the tree called "The Giving Tree"?

a) Because it gives everything it has to the boy

b) Because it takes a lot from the boy

c) Because it asks for a lot

d) Because it only provides shade

Answer: a) Because it gives everything it has to the boy

Q20 The story “The Giving Tree” mainly teaches about

a) Sacrifice and selflessness

b) Anger and revenge

c) Strength and power

d) Avoiding others

Answer: a) Sacrifice and selflessness

Chapter 15 – **Books**

Q1 What is the poem "Books" about?

a) The joy of reading books

b) Making books

c) Throwing books away

d) Selling books

Answer: a) The joy of reading books

Q2 How does the poet feel about books?

a) Excited and happy

b) Sad and bored

c) Scared

d) Angry

Answer: a) Excited and happy

Q3 According to the poem, books are a source of

a) Fun and learning

b) Fear

c) Confusion

d) Boredom

Answer: a) Fun and learning

Q4 What do books open up for the reader?

a) New worlds and adventures

b) Scary places

c) Empty spaces

d) Boring stories

Answer: a) New worlds and adventures

Q5 Books allow us to visit places

a) In our imagination

b) In reality

c) In our city

d) Only at school

Answer: a) In our imagination

Q6 How does reading books make us feel?

a) Curious and imaginative

b) Tired and bored

c) Angry and sad

d) Afraid

Answer: a) Curious and imaginative

Q7 Books can take us to

a) Magical lands and new places

b) Boring places

c) Dark caves

d) Empty rooms

Answer: a) Magical lands and new places

Q8 According to the poem, what do books bring to our lives?

a) Knowledge and joy

b) Anger

c) Boredom

d) Fear

Answer: a) Knowledge and joy

Q9 Books allow us to meet

a) Characters from different stories

b) Only our friends

c) Only our teachers

d) Only our family

Answer: a) Characters from different stories

Q10 The poem suggests that books are full of

a) Wonders and knowledge

b) Darkness and sadness

c) Fear and loneliness

d) Anger and frustration

Answer: a) Wonders and knowledge

Q11 Books are compared to

a) Adventures and journeys

b) Quiet places

c) Noisy machines

d) Heavy rocks

Answer: a) Adventures and journeys

Q12 The poem describes books as being

a) Magical and educational

b) Scary

c) Boring

d) Confusing

Answer: a) Magical and educational

Q13 Books are a source of

a) Endless stories and knowledge

b) Noise

c) Sleepiness

d) Anger

Answer: a) Endless stories and knowledge

Q14 The poem "Books" teaches us that reading

a) Opens up our mind to new things

b) Is very tiring

c) Should be avoided

d) Is only for school

Answer: a) Opens up our mind to new things

Q15 What do books encourage in readers?

a) Imagination and curiosity

b) Fear and sadness

c) Laziness

d) Frustration

Answer: a) Imagination and curiosity

Q16 The poet feels that books can take us

a) To magical and faraway places

b) Only to school

c) Only home

d) To places we dislike

Answer: a) To magical and faraway places

Q17 The poem encourages children to

a) Enjoy reading books

b) Avoid books

c) Tear books

d) Hide books

Answer: a) Enjoy reading books

Q18 What do books make possible according to the poem?

a) Discovering new ideas and places

b) Finding hidden toys

c) Becoming bored

d) Losing focus

Answer: a) Discovering new ideas and places

Q19 Why are books compared to adventures?

a) They offer exciting stories and knowledge

b) They are difficult to understand

c) They are old and dusty

d) They have no pictures

Answer: a) They offer exciting stories and knowledge

Q20 The poem “Books” celebrates

a) The joy and wonder of reading

b) The anger of losing a book

c) The confusion of studying

d) The fear of learning

Answer: a) The joy and wonder of reading

Chapter 16 - Going to Buy a Book

Q1 Who are the main characters in the story?

a) A brother and sister

b) Two friends

c) Two teachers

d) A mother and child

Answer: a) A brother and sister

Q2 Where are the children planning to go in the story?

a) To a bookshop

b) To school

c) To a library

d) To a garden

Answer: a) To a bookshop

Q3 Why do the children want to buy a book?

a) To enjoy reading it

b) For school homework

c) To gift to a friend

d) To give it to their teacher

Answer: a) To enjoy reading it

Q4 Who gives them money to buy the book?

a) Their mother

b) Their friend

c) Their teacher

d) Their uncle

Answer: a) Their mother

Q5 What type of book does the girl want to buy?

a) A thick book with stories

b) A book about animals

c) A very thin book

d) A picture book

Answer: a) A thick book with stories

Q6 What type of book does the boy want to buy?

a) A book with many pictures

b) A big novel

c) A book with no pictures

d) A science book

Answer: a) A book with many pictures

Q7 Who helps the children find the right book at the shop?

a) The bookseller

b) Their teacher

c) A friend

d) Their mother

Answer: a) The bookseller

Q8 How do the children feel at the bookshop?

a) Excited and happy

b) Sad

c) Confused

d) Angry

Answer: a) Excited and happy

Q9 What does the bookseller ask the children?

a) What kind of book they would like

b) If they have money

c) If they want a gift

d) If they know how to read

Answer: a) What kind of book they would like

Q10 How does the story show the children's interest in books?

a) By their excitement to buy books

b) By their dislike of the shop

c) By their dislike of reading

d) By their refusal to read

Answer: a) By their excitement to buy books

Q11 What do the children do after buying the books?

a) They start reading them immediately

b) They go back to the shop

c) They give them away

d) They lose the books

Answer: a) They start reading them immediately

Q12 The story teaches us the joy of

a) Choosing and reading books

b) Giving books as gifts

c) Collecting money

d) Buying toys

Answer: a) Choosing and reading books

Q13 What kind of books are available in the shop?

a) Books of all kinds

b) Only picture books

c) Only thick books

d) Only small books

Answer: a) Books of all kinds

Q14 The girl chooses a book with

a) Lots of stories

b) No pictures

c) Only science topics

d) Many games

Answer: a) Lots of stories

Q15 The boy chooses a book with

a) Lots of pictures

b) Only one story

c) No pictures

d) Many words

Answer: a) Lots of pictures

Q16 The children's visit to the bookshop shows that

a) They both have different tastes in books

b) They don't like reading

c) They don't have money

d) They dislike each other's choice

Answer: a) They both have different tastes in books

Q17 How do the children feel when they find the books they want?

a) Satisfied and happy

b) Sad

c) Annoyed

d) Confused

Answer: a) Satisfied and happy

Q18 The children's adventure at the bookshop teaches us that

a) Everyone has their own preferences in reading

b) All books are the same

c) It's difficult to find a good book

d) Reading is boring

Answer: a) Everyone has their own preferences in reading

Q19 What is one of the themes of the story?

a) The excitement of choosing books

b) The difficulty of reading

c) The confusion of buying gifts

d) The boredom of visiting a shop

Answer: a) The excitement of choosing books

Q20 The story "Going to Buy a Book" encourages children to

a) Appreciate the variety of books available

b) Buy only one type of book

c) Avoid reading

d) Collect only toys

Answer: a) Appreciate the variety of books available

Chapter 17 - The Naughty Boy

Q1 Who is the main character in the poem "The Naughty Boy"?

a) A mischievous boy

b) A strict teacher

c) A friendly girl

d) A wise old man

Answer: a) A mischievous boy

Q2 Where does the naughty boy travel to?

a) Scotland

b) America

c) Africa

d) India

Answer: a) Scotland

Q3 What is the naughty boy curious about in Scotland?

a) If things are different there

b) If it's very cold

c) If there are many animals

d) If it has many people

Answer: a) If things are different there

Q4 What does the boy discover about the ground in Scotland?

a) It is as hard as in England

b) It is very soft

c) It is made of water

d) It is blue in color

Answer: a) It is as hard as in England

Q5 What color is the Scottish ground, according to the boy?

a) Red

b) Blue

c) Green

d) Brown

Answer: d) Brown

Q6 What does the naughty boy find out about the Scottish sky?

a) It is as high as in England

b) It is much closer

c) It is very dark

d) It is very bright

Answer: a) It is as high as in England

Q7 What lesson does the naughty boy learn on his trip?

a) Things are often the same wherever we go

b) All places are different

c) It's better to stay home

d) Traveling is tiring

Answer: a) Things are often the same wherever we go

Q8 How does the naughty boy feel about his discoveries?

a) Surprised

b) Angry

c) Scared

d) Unhappy

Answer: a) Surprised

Q9 What does the naughty boy realize about himself after the trip?

a) That he is still the same

b) That he has changed

c) That he dislikes traveling

d) That he is scared

Answer: a) That he is still the same

Q10 The poem "The Naughty Boy" teaches us about

a) Finding similarities in new places

b) Always staying home

c) Being very serious

d) Disliking new things

Answer: a) Finding similarities in new places

Q11 What color is the Scottish sky according to the naughty boy?

a) Blue

b) Red

c) Green

d) Yellow

Answer: a) Blue

Q12 The boy realizes that the hills in Scotland are

a) Just as big as in England

b) Bigger

c) Smaller

d) Very steep

Answer: a) Just as big as in England

Q13 The poem shows the boy's surprise at discovering

a) Familiar things in a new place

b) New animals

c) A new language

d) Different plants

Answer: a) Familiar things in a new place

Q14 How does the poem describe the boy's adventure?

a) As a learning experience

b) As a scary journey

c) As a boring trip

d) As a hard lesson

Answer: a) As a learning experience

Q15 Why is the boy called "naughty"?

a) Because he is curious and adventurous

b) Because he dislikes others

c) Because he is rude

d) Because he doesn't study

Answer: a) Because he is curious and adventurous

Q16 The boy travels to Scotland to

a) See if things are different

b) Escape from school

c) Meet new people

d) Buy toys

Answer: a) See if things are different

Q17 How does the boy's trip end?

a) He returns with new understanding

b) He gets lost

c) He dislikes Scotland

d) He makes new friends

Answer: a) He returns with new understanding

Q18 The boy's experience in Scotland teaches readers that

a) Things can be similar even in different places

b) It's scary to travel

c) We should avoid exploring

d) All places are the same

Answer: a) Things can be similar even in different places

Q19 The naughty boy finds that people in Scotland

a) Speak like people in England

b) Look very different

c) Are very quiet

d) Don't like him

Answer: a) Speak like people in England

Q20 The poem "The Naughty Boy" encourages readers to

a) Be curious and explore new places

b) Avoid traveling

c) Stay at home always

d) Be afraid of strangers

Answer: a) Be curious and explore new places